The First Christmas
A Children's Bible Book

Allen Linn
Illustrations by Emily Zieroth

Copyright © 2020 by Allen Linn

Minneapolis, Minnesota

www.pyramidpublishers.com

All rights reserved. No part of this publication may be reproduced, stored in a retrieval system, or transmitted, in any form or by any means, electronic, mechanical, photocopying, recording, or otherwise, without the prior written permission of the author.

Printed by Lightning Source
1246 Heil Quaker Blvd.
La Vergne, TN USA 37086
ISBN – 978-1-7351068-1-6

Cover Design by Heidi Sutherlin, My Creative Pursuits
Illustrations by Emily Zieroth
Interior by Heidi Sutherlin, My Creative Pursuits
Printed in the United States of America

Unless otherwise noted, Scripture quotations are from The Holy Bible, New International Version^{tm}, NIV^{tm},
Copyright^C 1973, 1978, 1984, 2011 by Biblica, Inc.^{tm}
Used by permission of Zondervan

Dedication

This book is dedicated to two little girls named Desirae and Chloe who love to hear about Jesus.

For God so loved the world that he gave his one and only Son, that whoever believes in him shall not perish but have eternal life. (John 3:16)

God sent Jesus to earth so that all men, women, little boys, and little girls could get to heaven if they just make a choice to ask Him into their hearts and decide to follow Him. The time of His birth is called *The First Christmas*.

A long, long time ago, Old Testament prophets spoke of the coming Savior who would take away the sins of the world. In the book of Isaiah, we find:

For to us a child is born, to us a son is given, and the government will be on his shoulders. And He will be called Wonderful Counselor, Mighty God, Everlasting Father, Prince of Peace. (Isaiah 9:6)

His virgin birth was also prophesied, which means Jesus' Father was the Lord God Almighty and not a man.

Therefore the Lord Himself will give you a sign: the virgin shall be with child and will give birth to a son, and will call him Immanuel. (Isaiah 7:14)

Even the place of His birth (Bethlehem) is given:

But you Bethlehem Ephrathah, though you are small among the clans of Judah, out of you will come for me one who will be ruler over Israel, whose origins are from of old, from ancient times. (Micah 5:2)

At the appointed time (the First Christmas) Jesus took upon Himself humanity and came to earth. Luke 1:26-37 and 2:6-18 record the story.

God sent the angel Gabriel to Nazareth, a town in Galilee, to a virgin pledged to be married to a man named Joseph, a descendant of David. The virgin's name was Mary. The angel went to her and said, "Greetings, you who are highly favored! The Lord is with you."

Mary was greatly troubled at his words and wondered what kind of greeting this might be. But the angel said to her, "Do not be afraid, Mary, you have found favor with God. You will be with child and give birth to a Son, and you are to give Him the name Jesus. He will be great and will be called the Son of the Most High. The Lord God will give Him the throne of His father David, and He will reign over the house of Jacob forever; His kingdom will never end."

"How will this be?" Mary asked the angel.

The angel answered, "The Holy Spirit will come upon you, and the power of the Most High will overshadow you. So the Holy One to be born will be called the Son of God."

Matthew 1: 22 tells us,

She will give birth to a son, and you will give Him the name Jesus, because He will save His people from their sins. All this took place to fulfill what the Lord had said through the prophet: "The virgin shall be with child, and will give birth to a son, and they will call him Immanuel" (which means, "God with us").

The Apostle John, inspired by the Holy Spirit of God, tells why Jesus came to earth and who He really was. We can find this in the first chapter of the Gospel of John.

In the beginning was the Word, and the Word was with God, and the Word was God. He was with God in the beginning. Through Him all things were made; without Him nothing was made that has been made. In Him was life, and that life is the light of men. The light shines in the darkness, but the darkness has not understood it.

The true light that gives light to every man was coming into the world. He was in the world, and though the world was made through Him, the world did not recognize Him. He came to that which was His own, but His own did not receive Him. Yet to all who received Him, to those who believed in His name, He gave the right to become children of God – children born not of natural descent, or of human decision or a husbands will, but born of God.

The Word became flesh and made His dwelling among us.

In other words, the Son of God stepped out of heaven and into our world on that First Christmas.

During her pregnancy, Mary and Joseph had to walk for a week to Joseph's hometown of Bethlehem to register in a national census (counting all the people of a country). The little town was filled with travelers, and there was no room for Mary and Joseph in the inns. So they had to stay in a stable for animals.

The baby's crib (manger) was probably a cattle feeding trough filled with hay. Swaddling clothes or blankets, used to wipe down the animals, were used as His bedding. It would have smelled awful and the filthy stable would have been filled with flies, hardly a fitting place for the King of kings and Lord of lords.

As the Apostle Paul reminds us,

For you know the grace of our Lord Jesus Christ, that though He was rich, yet for your sakes he became poor, so that you through His poverty might become rich (2 Corinthians 8:9).

His life started with no room in the inn, and many people of the time rejected Him.

He was in the world, and though the world was made through Him, the world did not recognize Him. He came to that which was His own, but His own did not receive Him (John 1:11).

The good news is that many did receive Him.

Yet to all who did receive Him, to those who believed in His name, He gave the right to become the children of God – children born not of natural descent, nor of human decision, nor a husband's will, but born of God (John 1:12-13).

Jesus was born in Bethlehem where shepherds were tending their flocks in nearby fields. They were in the fields all night because it was the season when the lambs gave birth. The True Lamb of God was born when the lambs were being born.

Thus, in the little town of Bethlehem, one silent night while the world slept, the One who stepped out of eternity into time was born of the Virgin Mary. And angels announced His Arrival to a lowly band of shepherds.

Luke 2:9-16 tells the story of that First Christmas:

An angel of the Lord appeared to them, and the glory of the Lord shone around them, and they were terrified. But the angel said to them, "Do not be afraid. I bring you good news that will cause great joy for all the people. Today in the town of David a Savior has been born to you; he is the Messiah, the Lord. This will be a sign to you: You will find a baby wrapped in cloths and lying in a manger."

Suddenly a great company of the heavenly host appeared with the angel, praising God and saying,

"Glory to God in the highest heaven,
and on earth peace to those on whom his favor rests."

When the angels had left them and gone into heaven, the shepherds said to one another, "Let's go to Bethlehem and see this thing that has happened, which the Lord has told us about."

So they hurried off and found Mary and Joseph, and the baby, who was lying in the manger.

In Matthew Chapter 2:1-2, we are told of wise men from the east who came to visit the baby Jesus.

After Jesus was born in Bethlehem in Judea, during the time of King Herod, Magi from the east came to Jerusalem and asked, "Where is the one who has been born king of the Jews? We saw his star when it rose and have come to worship him."

They might have come from Babylon, which was east of Jerusalem across the Syrian Desert. When they saw His star, they knew when to start their journey. The star they followed was a special star made for this purpose, a supernatural light going before them pointing out the exact spot of the supernatural birth.

The purpose of the first Christmas (the birth of Jesus) was to take us to Good Friday (His crucifixion) and from there to Easter (His glorious resurrection). These are the three most important events in His life.

A very important Christian author from the 20th Century, C.S. Lewis, summed it up very well: "The Son of God became the Son of Man, that the sons of men might become the sons of God." You are a son or daughter of your father and mother, but you can also be a son or daughter of God if you invite Jesus into your heart.

The Creator of the whole world (including little you) entered human history to suffer and die for sinful humanity. This is the glorious message of the Gospel: mankind, separated from God through sin, can become the children of God through Jesus Christ.

Those tiny hands that clung to Mary once created the universe and later would be stretched out on a cross and nails driven through them. It was on the cross that God placed the sins of the world on Jesus and judged Him for all of us. God is holy and God is love. His holiness demanded that our sins be paid for, while His love carried this out through His Son, Jesus Christ. Thus, the symbol of Christmas is not merely a manger but a blood-stained cross and an empty tomb.

Jesus humbled Himself to be born in a stable and to labor in Joseph's carpenter shop. He removed His robes of glory and put on the clothes of a carpenter. In heaven, the angels greatest joy was to serve Jesus' every desire. But on earth, He became the servant of all.

[Jesus] did not come to be served, but to serve, and to give his life as a ransom for many (Matthew 20:28).

The people of Jesus' day mistakenly thought that the Messiah would come like a king in all His glory and restore Israel's worldly kingdom. But His mission was to establish a spiritual kingdom, not a worldly one. In His outward appearance, Jesus was a poor carpenter born into a poor family and lived in a poor town. In truth, He was the Messiah, who came from the family of David, but He did not appear so.

Jesus humbled Himself still further by being obedient to the point of death. All the world's men and women die because we are sinners and have no choice, but Christ's death was a choice, an act of obedience to the Father. This was so different from Adam who disobeyed a simple command in the Garden of Eden not to eat from one of many trees. Jesus, referred to as the Second Adam, sacrificed His life for us on a Roman cross, for the redemption of our sins, so we could spend eternity with Him and His Father in Heaven. He died for the salvation of all the men, women, little boys, and little girls who accept Him as their Savior and Lord. What a wonderful gift. That's why we love Jesus so much.

Who was this Jesus?

The Scriptures are clear concerning Jesus eternal existence and His taking on humanity to suffer and die on the cross for our sins:

Who being in the very nature of God, did not consider equality with God something to be grasped, but made of Himself nothing, taking the very nature of a servant, being made in human likeness. And being found in appearance as a man, He humbled Himself and became obedient to death – even death on a cross (Philippians 2:6-8).

From eternity past, He knew He would come to suffer and die. The prophet Isaiah told us about Jesus many years before that First Christmas.

Who has believed our message and to whom has the arm of the Lord been revealed? He grew up before Him like a tender shoot, and like a root out of dry ground…A man of sorrows, and familiar with suffering.…

Surely, He took up our infirmities and carried our sorrows…He was crushed for our iniquities; the punishment that brought us peace was upon him, and by his wounds, we are healed (Isaiah 53:1-5).

Hebrews 1:6 tells us that when Jesus came to earth, the angels worshipped Him:

And again when God brings His Firstborn into the world, He says, "Let all God's angels worship Him."

And Hebrews 2:14-17 says:

Since the children have flesh and blood, He too shared in their humanity so that by His death He might destroy him who holds the power of death – that is the devil – and free those who all their lives were held in slavery by the fear of death. For surely it is not angels he helps, but Abraham's descendants. For this reason He had to be made like His brothers in every way, in order that He might become a merciful and faithful High Priest in service to God and that He might make atonement for the sins of the people.

This is the heart of Christianity. He left His position of being served to become a servant as He said to His disciples:

The Son of Man did not come to be served, but to serve, and to give His life as a ransom for many (Matthew 20:28).

During His ministry, Jesus told His disciples why He had come to earth – to die for the sins of the world and be resurrected so all men, women, little boys, and little girls could go to heaven if they asked Jesus into their hearts.

From that time on Jesus began to explain to His disciples that He must go to Jerusalem and suffer many things at the hands of the elders, chief priests and teachers of the law, that He must be killed and on the third day be raised to life (Matthew 16:21).

When they came together in Galilee, He said to them, "The Son of Man is going to be betrayed into the hands of men. They will kill him, and on the third day he will be raised to life," and the disciples were filled with grief (Matthew 17:22-23).

Before being arrested in the Garden of Gethsemane, Jesus prayed to His Father in Heaven.

Father, the hour has come. Glorify your Son, that your Son may glorify you. For you granted him authority over all people that he might give eternal life to all those you have given him. Now this is eternal life: that they know you, the only true God, and Jesus Christ, whom you have sent. I have brought you glory on earth by finishing the work you gave me to do. And now, Father, glorify me in your presence with the glory I had with you before the world began (John 17:1-5).

With these words, Jesus allowed Himself to be arrested by a bunch of soldiers and Jewish officials. It was the beginning of the marvelous gift God gave us for our redemption.

Jesus was suffering as God's sacrificial Lamb for the sins of the world. It was not what men did to Him but what He suffered at the hand of God, which led Him to cry out, *My God, my God, why have you forsaken me?* He was forsaken that we might find acceptance. He thirsted so that we could drink the water of life.

He bore the curse we deserved. This is the heart of the message of the cross and reconciliation to God:

But we preach Christ and Him crucified: a stumbling block to the Jews and foolishness to the Gentiles, but to those whom God has called, both Jews and Greeks (Gentiles), Christ is the power of God and the wisdom of God (1 Corinthians 1:23-24).

He was God taking upon Himself humanity to become our representative, our Kinsman Redeemer. As mankind's representative, He took our sins upon Himself and was judged by God in our place as though He had actually committed all the sins of humanity.

He was pierced for our sorrows, He was crushed for our iniquities, the punishment that brought us peace was upon Him, and by His wounds we are healed. We all, like sheep, have gone astray, each of us has turned to their own way; and the Lord has laid on Him the iniquity of us all. He was oppressed and afflicted, yet He did not open His mouth; He was led like a lamb to the slaughter (Isaiah 43:4-7).

He was born for the purpose of dying. *Like a lamb led to the slaughter.* His whole life on earth was lived in the shadow of the cross. He was the Passover Lamb to be killed as our sacrifice for sin. As He told His disciples:

For the Son of Man came to seek and to save what was lost (Luke 19:10).

Christ Jesus came into the world to save sinners (1 Timothy 1:15).

God transformed the cross, an instrument of horror and agonizing execution, into an instrument of love and mercy.

By faith, believers, conscious of their sin and guilt, and of Christ being their Substitute, accept God's provision and allow God to roll all their sinful guilt and shame unto Christ their Substitute. Thus, Christ's righteousness is given to sinners. That's what it means to accept Jesus into your heart.

This very day, today, Jesus stands at the door of your heart and knocks:

Here I am! I stand at the door and knock. If anyone hears my voice and opens the door, I will come in and eat with that person, and they with me. (Revelation 3:20).

When we open the door and invite Jesus into our hearts, we have a new relationship with God through faith in Christ's work on the cross. Jesus inviting Himself in to have dinner with us demonstrates the kind of relationship He wants to have with us – a meal between friends. We with Him and He with us. This is what it means to be *In Christ*:

Therefore if anyone is in Christ, he is a new creation; the old has gone, the new has come" (2 Corinthians 5:17).

This is what we celebrate at Christmas: the birth of Jesus who took on humanity and lifted us from the depths of sin to the height of becoming the children of God.

How great is the love the Father has lavished upon us, that we should be called the children of God! (1 John 3:1).

This is why Jesus is called the reason for the Christmas season.

www.ingramcontent.com/pod-product-compliance
Lightning Source LLC
Chambersburg PA
CBHW042032100526
44587CB00029B/4392